TEXT BOMB

EXPLOSIVE
WRITING
FROM

0010

EDITED BY
TRACEY ICETON

Published by Sixth Element Publishing
on behalf of SRC Bede 6th Form

ISBN 978-1-908299-09-3

British Library Cataloguing in Publication Data. A catalogue record for this book is available from the British Library.

Printed in Great Britain.

Sixth Element Publishing
Arthur Robinson House
13-14 The Green
Billingham TS23 1EU
Tel: 01642 360253
www.6epublishing.net

Designed by Matt Fodor

CONTENTS

FOREWORD

0010 are a crack squad, specially chosen for their diverse writing skills, for a dangerous mission that others would baulk at: to produce an anthology of only the very best prose and poetry imaginable.

Assembled in 2010 and consisting of ten members, 0010 chose to accept this mission and embrace the challenge set out before them. As the work published here explodes into the ether there can be no doubt that they have triumphed in the face of adversity, overcoming all the dangers of their mission; writing, reading, editing, rewriting, rereading, writing some more. These hazards conquered they have succeeded in produced a range of writing that is elegant, thought-provoking, challenging, humorous and moving.

The text contained in this dossier is marked confidential. Only those with the highest level of security clearance are entitled to read these pages and, while what you find here may astonish, shock, amuse or even haunt you for the rest of your days you, as one of the strictly limited number of officials entitled to access this report, are charged with the task of enjoying the work in here to the fullest letter of the law. Do not shirk your duty.

Before you turn the pages that follow I think it only fair to warn you that 0010 do not accept any responsibility for injury or damage resulting from the reading of their work. Should you split your sides laughing at the antics of "Dauntless Dave", find your vision becoming blurry with tears at Mickey's tragic story in "The Beauty of the Human Race" or feel your heart palpitating with tension and fear as you get into the taxi in "Backseat Driver" 0010 would remind you that you HAVE BEEN WARNED!

Any attempt to discredit, slander or otherwise defame the writing in this document will be considered an act of treason and is punishable by dismemberment with a blunt pencil. Remember, 0010 are the elite, they have succeeded where others did not even dare tread. You cross them at your peril!

T

ON THE EDGE

BY STEPH MITCHELL

She thought you cared
You were there when she cried
So where were you the night that she died?
It was all your fault
And you didn't even realise
The pain you caused reflected in her eyes.

She took a chance on you
And never did anything wrong
Like love described in a Taylor Swift song.
You were so close
And you couldn't even see
You and she were simply meant to be.

She saw you the other week
She knew you wouldn't try
She said to herself "this is the last tear I'll cry"
So she went home
That last tear in her eye
She felt so alone she just wanted to die.

She went to the kitchen
And pulled out a knife
She wrote on her arm just one word: Life
What was the point?
It could all go away
But mother was home she'd have to hide it all day.

A new cut every day
Months passed and you didn't care
To be honest you didn't realise they were there.
A year or two later
And look who she has become
You abandoned the mess – oh what have you done?

You spoke to her on that day
You told her that she mattered
You were too late; her heart was already shattered.
She waved goodbye
Oh but if you only knew
Her final note would be addressed to you.

"A girl on the edge,
So this is the final part,
I guess you never realised but you stole my heart.
I'm sorry for the pain
I'm sorry for leaving a bloody knife,
I'm sorry that I messed up your bloody life."

Daddy's Girl By Amy Holmes

I hear my friend Judy knocking at the door. Stuffing the remainders of my toast into my mouth, I hop off my chair and head to the door. Daddy stops me. He opens his arms, beckoning me closer, his eyes shimmering with love.

"Where's my kiss, then?" he asks.

I obediently make my way back to him, raising onto my tiptoes to kiss his whiskery cheek. His arms form a cage around me.

He's such a kind daddy. He loves me so much. He's the loveliest, kindest, nicest daddy in the whole world.

It was hard for him, after Mummy left, but he took such good care of me. He would brush and plait my hair without pulling even once. He would fasten the buttons on my cardigan properly. He would bathe me on a night and change me into my pyjamas, and if I ever had a nasty dream he would slither into my bed and let me cuddle up to him and make things all better.

Judy has a boy she likes. I suppress my smirk. She's so silly, really. So stupid. Stupid, stupid Judy. She thinks she likes Aaron because he's funny and clever and has freckles the exact shade of his sandy hair scattered across his nose. I'm older than that. I know why men and women really like each other. I know where *babies* come from. Daddy told me. He's so clever, my daddy. He's the loveliest, kindest, nicest daddy in the whole world.

Judy gets quiet as we approach the school. It's been quiet since last week, when Daniel went away. They found him in a ditch on the beach, all bloated and red. We had an assembly for him at school, and everyone cried for a long time. Nobody cried when I got red.

I didn't understand why everyone was so upset. Daniel was a horrible little boy. He picked his nose and ate it, and he kicked a football at me once when I was skipping. He was stupid too. He hadn't thought it strange at all when I asked him to go for a walk with me after school. He thought I *liked* him.

In the playground, Ashley and Abigail start crying, so Judy starts too. She perks up immediately when school is over, though. We go for a walk. Her blonde curls begin to look more and more like wool, and her endless chatter grows louder and higher until she is simply bleating annoyingly in my ear, saying all sort of nasty, whispery things.

Like, *I love you.*

Like, *my precious little girl.*

Like, *you can't tell anyone.*

She's the loveliest, kindest, nicest friend in the whole world.

I point out towards to sea.

"Look over there."

Judy squints. Leans forward.

It doesn't take much. Just a little push.

She screams all the way down. When the screams stop, I carefully edge towards where she fell.

I can see her at the bottom, small and twisted and red all over. Like a crushed ant.

For a moment I think about following her. But not yet. Not yet. Daddy would worry. I was already late.

I'd scraped my knees at playtime. They were all dirty. He'd have to give me a bath again.

FINALLY. By Helen Daly

Finally, I can be who I want to be.
Finally, I'm where I wanted to be.
No more pretending to be, to love, to enjoy.
Why should he control me?
It's only a ring; why should it stop my heart from skipping?

When he was around, no one heard my song.
Now, I sing from the highest peak, in the highest note.
My thoughts have been released; my voice is no longer caged.
My soul can run free, free to enjoy the sun, the moon, the stars.
Time can wait for me!

Rules? They no longer apply to me.
Why should they?
My mind can wander to its own rhythm.
There's no need to scrape my feet in the abyss, I can stride into the light!
Finally, I can be who I want to be.

Compulsive Liar

Today, it has been thirteen years, six months and four hours since my guardian angel first visited me. Yes, I have a guardian angel. If you don't believe me, there's a few newspaper clippings about it and you can ask my mum, if you really want to. You should believe me, though. I know I don't always tell the truth - nobody does - but have I ever lied to you? Think about it for a minute. If you'll listen to me, I'll tell you all about it.

A few days before Christmas all those years ago, I was a three year old child. Picture me, with two red pigtails and a toothy smile, wandering a busy shopping centre. My dad is holding tight onto my hand, but I'm restless. There's so much to see that my little mind can't quite process everything; one minute there's a picture book in the window that I want more than anything else, then the next minute there's a doll in someone's arms that I just have to touch. And at the centre of all of this, where an impatient crowd has gathered, is Santa's Grotto.

Dad promises me more than once that we can visit, but first we have to finish shopping. I walk obediently by his side for what feels like an age, but soon I am frustrated enough to scream, right there in a knot of people. Dad is holding up something pink and purple with a perplexed look on his face; by the time he turns to ask what I think, I am lost in the crowd.

I feel a pang of fear as I leave my Dad, but it's just so irritating, watching everybody walk past me weighed down with the things I want. I wander further away from the shop and my dad, feeling braver with every step. I don't walk very far, but it feels like at least a mile to Santa's Grotto. I love my dad and don't want to run away or anything, but it really is important that I speak to Santa before Christmas. If Dad doesn't finish shopping until late, then there's a chance I won't be able to go... and I have the feeling that my dad isn't taking this seriously enough. If Santa doesn't know what I want, how am I ever going to get it?

I walk right up to where the people are queuing, and I stand in line behind two girls and their mother; the girls are twins, and I remember thinking how eerily similar they looked. They both have the same clothes, too, right down to their frilly white socks and pink braces. Their mother looks concerned when she sees I am alone, and asks me where my mother is.

"It's alright," a voice says suddenly, from somewhere behind us. "She's with me." I turned around, expecting to see Dad, but it is a strange man with stubble on his face and a purple shirt. Before I have a chance to say anything to the contrary, he lunges forward and seizes my arm, guiding me away from the crowd.

"I don't know you," I tell him, fighting his hold on me, "Get off!"

"No," the man counters, lifting me over his shoulder in a fireman's lift, "You're coming with me."

He says, "Now be quiet, okay? I'm a friend. I'm your Mummy's friend," and it is then that I see Dad, fighting his way through the throng of shoppers. He's seen me!

But the man notices Dad too, and he starts running. I shriek and shout, "Dad!" but nobody so much as asks if I am all right. They just go on with their shopping as though nothing is happening, as if a three year old isn't being abducted in front of their very eyes. Dad chases the man all the way to the doors of the shopping centre but remains a good distance away; Dad is older than my captor, and far more unfit. He doesn't stand a chance.

Dad stops to alert the security staff as we leave through the double doors, then he runs after us again and climbs into his car. The strange man doesn't seem troubled by this; in fact, his eyes gleam with a kind of quiet enjoyment. He revs up the engine then speeds away from the car park quickly, two security men running towards us just that little bit too late. We pull away onto the motorway, and that is where my memory stops.

The newspaper clippings say that we crashed into a bush just two miles away from the shopping centre. Luckily it was a small road, so there was no-one else about. And I had had the foresight (even as a three year old) to strap myself in, so I was barely harmed. My captor, though, was badly hurt. Dad told the police that he limped away from the scene of the crash as though his ankle was broken; that when he ran after him his clothes were torn in places, and he was bleeding from a deep cut above his eye.

Dad got pretty close to him, but the man seemed mad and Dad was mostly concerned with getting me checked out. He called an ambulance and tried to get the man to stay so the police could talk to him, but he got away. I was fine, but the man was not. He was never found again, but here's the thing; I know what happened to him. I honest-to-God do.

He's dead. I know he is. They haven't found a body, but they will, eventually. Just give it time. And if you want to know how I know, well, there's no easy way to tell you this, but I see him, sometimes. In my dreams. He's always there, somewhere behind my eyelids. Sometimes when I am in that dim, dreary half-place between sleeping and waking, I see him. And he sees me. We talk, sometimes.

And there, there it is! That shift in the way you look at me, like you're embarrassed. I'm telling the truth, I swear! And if you don't believe me, then that's your problem. But I honestly thought you would.

I'll be fine without you. I'll always be fine. I'm destined for great things, you know; he sometimes tells me that on the cold nights when I can't quite seem to drift off. I remember his face though it's been thirteen years; how could I remember if I were lying? And he says he'll protect me, until I'm old and wrinkled. He says I've got great things to come in this life, and I can't wait to find out what they are.

By Jenny Bate

Hansel and Gretel By Anna Twizell

Section of Case 8 - Account by Mary Witchington
Questions by Thomas Underwood

So here I lie, covered in burns. I feel terrible. All ze beeping around me iz very off putting too. I cannot think straight. I vill tell you ze things I remember from before I got here Mr. Policeman, though you must understand, my memory iz hazy.

I was decorating my kitchen, sinze my poor husband died I've been doing up all of ze rooms. So there I vaz, minding my own business, painting ze valls a sweet terracotta, when I heard ze excited little voices of children outside. I peered around my kitchen window to find ze idiots eating avay at my newly decorated cottage. You can just imagine my despair. I wazn't sure whezer to run out there and smack zem with my broom. Zere were two of zem, both little porky children. A boy and a girl. Ze boy in tight green lederhosen, ze girl squeezed into an orange and blue pleated dress. Zey were hideous. Both with chunky pale faces and bright blonde hair. I vould put zem at about 8 year old perhaps. My house is beautiful too, and zey were ruining it!

The boy waz scraping huge handfuls of pink butter cream from my drainpipe and forcing it straight into hiz mouth, while ze girl leaned forward to lick the liquorish vindowpane. I had had enough! Sinze I had the exterior of the cottage done last month, it has attracted a lot of the local kiddies and I am sick of it. Especially because I live in ze deepest darkest part of ze forest, zey shouldn't even be in zis area. I vent out to scare them away but they didn't appear to be afraid of me.

I asked zem what zey were doing, but all zey could keep telling me was how hungry zey both vere and zat zeir parents had abandoned them in ze forest with only some bread between them. Vell, my heart just melted zere and zen. Zese poor poor children, all alone in ze deep dark wood. And I guess zey veren't actually that hideous, in hindsight, zey just needed to be neatened up a little. So naturally my maternal instincts took over and I hurried zem inside, promising to make zem a feast like zey had never seen. I gave zem both some of my husband's old clothes to change into, so zey no longer looked like zey were about to burst out. Wearing my husband's old lumberjack shirts zey almost looked cute. I decided it vas my right, no, my duty to look after zese children. Seems zeir parents hadn't bothered.

I set to work straight away in the kitchen. I cooked zem trout with garlic, bratwurst and cheese, zen doughnut platter for desert. Yet even after zis zey insisted zey were still hungry. Although I had grown fond of zem, zey were terrible greedy little children.

Oh, I haven't told you their names yet have I? The young man was Hansel, a very bright child, if not a little devious. And Gretel waz my girl, I thought she would turn into a lovely lady some day. Make a man a very good wife. I just knew it.

So vere was I? Yes zat's it, the zree of us spent a few very happy days together. Until something changed, I ran out of food and it's like zey turned on me. Zey went outside and began to help zemselves once again to the sweets on my cottage. Hansel vas taking large bites of gingerbread from my walls, and Gretel vas picking out the gummy bears from my hanging baskets. And oh gosh, it's all coming back to me now. I shouted at zem, zen suddenly they both spread evil grins across zeir fat faces. I shouted more, telling zem to go home, zat I didn't vant them here, I slammed the door on zem. Oh no. I made them angry didn't I?

I remember I went back to the kitchen to vash up but zey had already forced their porky bodies through my open vindow. I remember it all clearly now, Hansel pulled the oven door open vide, vhilst Gretel pushed me with all of her might into ze oven. Zat is where I got all of zese burns. I wish I had never opened my door to them in the first place. I will make zose idiots pay for zis.

MAKING HEADLINES

I see the church; the spire
twists high in the morning
sky.
I'm getting closer.
He told me he would wait
outside the little, quaint
souvenir shop, opposite the
church.
He has planned a lovely day
 - a walk round the shops,
picnic; how romantic!
I hate that.

I've just cut through the
trees; the rabbits ran from
me.
The trees are thinning out.
Now I'm on the cold, hard
path.
Just a few more turns, then
I'm there.

I grew up here.
One of the lucky ones actually
- I'm lucky because I
don't live here now.
Too boring, too quiet.
I need excitement.
Thanks to me, this town will
be alive with flashes and
recordings - maybe even a
tribute!
I'm going to be a star!

One more turn… there he is!
The streets are empty…
…like his heart.
His back is to me, slouching.
I hate it when he slouches.
His dark hair is rustling.
He turns around, I hide.
He must not see me.
He faces the church again.
I continue to creep along
the wall…
My long white dress is
trailing.
I'm right behind him…
"Hello dear…"

He has no chance of
returning a bittersweet
greeting.

He is on the floor, the
ruby liquid flows on to my
dress.
It drips from the silver.
It has made my own red
carpet.
I walk down it.
Now, I wait.
Wait for the sirens… the
flashes… the fame.

by Helen Daly

Invisible by Steph Mitchell

You don't know who I really am
the girl I am inside
the one who abuses a mask
the girl who always hides.

The girl in the street
always looking down
the one you bully
the one who never
utters a sound.

SKIN BY ALEX HARKER

The millions of molecules melted into one,
Have craved that sweet touch for so long
Hoping for passion, for love and for lust
Waiting for that teasing bite or soft touch.

The skin meets and melts into one
Starting a chemical reaction that's so strong.
All the doubt, and fears just seem to go away
Because this one night, I can enjoy you my way.

RAPUNZEL

By Anna Twizell

Looking back now, many many years ago,
Into the old past that I used to know,
I lived in a little cottage up on a hill,
Just down the lane from dear Jack and Jill.
In a town so beautiful, with all flowers wild,
I knew a young couple, trying for a child.
They were a darling sweet man and wife,
They certainly made complete each other's life,
Together they longed and hoped for a baby girl,
With big blue eyes and hair that would curl.
They were the happiest pair that I ever knew,
They were perfect together and their wish came true,
Fairly late on in the months of nine,
For her condition she was feeling quite fine.
All except her strange cravings for peas,
When she didn't have them she would drop to her knees.
Yet she was so desperate she just cried and cried.
Seeing her distress her husband tried,
He decided to climb the garden wall,
It was quite a struggle although he was tall,
By the light of the moon he saw rows of green,
Cabbage, leek, broccoli and bean.
Now dear reader, I must remind you,
It's a sin to steal, but give him his due,
He didn't want to do it, he didn't think he should,
But he loved his wife so dearly, he felt he was doing good.
His eyes then fell on his wife's sacred treat,
He crept toward the peas, his footsteps were neat,
When lights flooded the garden from the door ajar!
And the couple's old neighbour yelled an, 'Arghhh!'
'I have caught you now trying to steal,
I am an old lady, this is quite an ordeal,
To make up for this theft you will repay me by
Giving me your daughter before her first cry!'
The man felt magic, as though under a spell,
He began to smile and nod his head as well.
See dear reader, you must understand this glitch,
Their ugly old neighbour was actually a witch!

With frizzy straw hair, and the ugliest face,
Covered in boils with skin the colour of paste.
Then came the time, when the child was born,
And the poor couple had to hand her to the nasty crone,
For the next twelve years the baby grew,
In the care of the witch, her parents she never knew.
Yet they remembered, and they wept every day,
About the time when they had given their precious babe away.
The witch knew the parents had stolen before,
And she feared the day they would knock at her door,
So she relocated the girl, to a tower so high,
At the windows she lived, she was right in the sky,
Stuck all on her own in a room that was plain,
She misunderstood why things couldn't stay the same.
Now dear reader, you must catch on,
There is another jump in time before my story is done.
So five years later, when the girl was seventeen,
In the tower she was locked, as beautiful as a queen,
With a fair pale complexion and long golden hair,
Daydreaming she spent her days, alone with no care.
One bright day she stood at her window and sang,
She had a fine voice, with a slight southern twang,
And a prince who was riding his horse in the woods,
Galloped quick to the tower, to hear more of the goods.
When his eyes fell on our young maiden, Rapunzel by name,
He knew there and then that his life wouldn't be the same.
For he suddenly felt that he must be in love,
With our sweet heroine, his beauty from above.
He then shouted to her, 'Please throw down your hair!
For you are too perfect, I must get up there!'
In an instant she threw down her long golden locks,
For him to climb up the tower, and rescue her from her box.
And this is the part where they shared their first kiss,
I won't go into detail, but for them it was bliss.
So reader, if this was the end of my story, all would seem well,
But I think you have realised, it is now time to dwell.
The wicked witch then appeared, in a puff of smoke,
The prince was astounded, he thought it must be joke.

But on this particular day she was feeling rather mean,
She told him that his break in was terribly obscene!
'You will not steal my daughter! Do you really think you can?
I hate your type of person, you silly little man!'
And after this she charged and pushed him with all of her might,
Backwards he stumbled out of the window into his fatal flight.
So my dear reader, is there a lesson to be learnt?
Never steal or force entry if you don't want to get hurt.
For our charming handsome prince, he got to feel true love,
Before his new lover's mother then gave him the shove.
Was his death uncalled for? Was it possibly fate?
Whatever you decide your answer is, it is now too late
For poor fair Rapunzel, she sits in the tower still,
People say she's mad, all she does is sing at the window sill.
Before the witch left her, she cut her hair into a bob,
To protect her from future men and another heart throb.
And as for my sweet young couple, who are getting on now,
In their lives they've had more sadness than anyone should allow,
They spend their days together, sewing shirt sleeves and hats,
And as a treat on the weekend they groom their twenty seven cats.

Trapped

by Steph Mitchell

Poor little princess,
so perfect and petite
dressed in her finest
while locked in her keep.

Pretty teenage royalty
perfect and poised
living in her castle prison
a life of pure white noise.

GOD PLEASE HELP MY BROTHER by Amy Holmes

Even through my iPod earphones, I heard the front door slam. It had to be Syed, storming out for what must have been the fifth time that week. I could hear Dad shouting after him. He could scream until he was blue in the face, but we all knew that Syed wouldn't be back tonight. Maybe not even tomorrow night.

It all started about a year ago, and crept up on me so slowly that I hadn't even realised what was happening until I saw it with my own eyes. Syed had always been so wonderful to me. He was more than my brother – he was my best friend, too. When I was little he would squeeze into my play house with me and play mummies and daddies, giving my Barbie dolls funny squeaky voices and making them dance around the cups and saucers of my tea set. He would plait my hair for me and paint my nails every colour of the rainbow without ever smudging the polish. He taught me how to read and draw and play the recorder. I was convinced for a very long time that Syed was magic. He made everything come alive.

I was completely convinced that things would stay the same forever. Even when I started secondary school, Syed was there, threatening to beat up the boys who had sworn at me and called me a Paki because of my hajib. I even believed that he would beat people up for me despite the fact that he was short and a little on the pudgy side.

It was when Syed started college that things began to change and I was forced to face the harsh reality that the world did not, in fact, revolve around me. Suddenly he didn't have time for me. He didn't have time for any of us. He wanted to be with his friends.

Well, friend. A friend that wasn't me.

Connor wasn't what Mum would call a respectable boy. He was moody and sarcastic and had scars on his knuckles from fighting. I had seen him kicking the stuffing out of more than one person on more than one occasion. Syed had kept well away from him in secondary; everyone had. But after a fateful Geology lesson, that was it, Syed was infatuated. It was always Connor this, Connor that; I had to bite the insides of my cheeks raw to stop myself shouting "What about me? Don't I matter any more?" It had always been Syed and me. And suddenly it wasn't.

Syed and Dad started butting heads about eight months ago, and it had only gotten worse since then. I couldn't understand. Out of the two of us, Syed had always been the kinder, the gentler, the more obedient. The favourite. His grades couldn't compare to mine, he was bad at sports and was banned from using any and all kitchen appliances ever since that one particularly memorable microwave disaster last year... but somehow I always ended up in second place. Syed was Mummy's Little Miracle: she had been wrongly diagnosed as infertile a year before his birth. She wasn't the only one to believe he could do no wrong, either;

from the moment I could open my eyes and stretch out my tiny starfish hands for him to hold, I was smitten. I decided a long time ago that I didn't mind coming second to him. So I couldn't understand the change.

It was just little things at first: eating with his knife and fork in the wrong hands, playing his music too loudly, talking back once too often. But they built up, like a tightly sealed bottle of pop being shaken rigorously.

Syed said he didn't want to go to the Mosque any more. Dad exploded. He hit Syed. Made his nose bleed. Even he was shocked – he'd never raised a hand to either of us before. Syed had put on a brave face, but I heard him sniffling in his bed late that night. I slid under his duvet and snuggled up to him; his face was hot with tears. He wrapped an arm around me and hugged me tight. His body wasn't as soft as it used to be. He had lost weight. I told myself it was a good thing.

"Please stop this," I begged. "I want things back to normal."

Syed waited a long time before replying, "Okay, Maria. If that's what you want."

But it didn't stop. He kept seeing Connor, and Dad kept hitting him, shouting "You disrespect me! You disrespect your mother!" Mum would send me to my room, but even hidden under my bed with my fingers in my ears, I could hear every word. I shuddered at the thought of Dad's huge, hairy hands coming down again and again on my brother. His grades fell from Cs to Us. It only added fuel to Dad's rage. And with every stinging slap and every purple bruise, I could feel Syed slipping further and further away from me, and Mum, and Dad.

It was only when Syed hit back that Dad realised there was nothing he could do.

He took to spending whole nights away from the house. The only person he would answer his mobile to was me, and it was always the same thing – he was spending the night at Connor's. No big deal. He'd be back in the morning.

He was like a different person over the phone. His voice was lighter, and I could hear his smile. The weight of Dad's fists had been lifted, and he was so happy. So happy with Connor. That made me angry. I was the only one struggling. I still needed Syed so much, and he didn't need me at all.

Mum was the only one who could really get through to him. After Dad had finished with him and stalked off to the garden shed to calm down, too exhausted to swing his fists or his feet any more, Mum would step in. She would kneel down next to Syed and hold him to her chest and cry and call him her baby, her precious baby. Syed would cry too, sometimes. Then he would sit her down and make her a cup of tea and promise her all sorts of empty, impossible things.

Syed had long since stopped noticing my tears.

I couldn't even escape from it at school. The boys would make horrible remarks, and they all whittled down to Connor.

"Your brother's a faggot," they would say. "Everyone knows he's shagging his best mate."

"No, he's not!" I would shout back. They didn't know what they were talking about. Syed wasn't like that. He was the purest person I knew. Connor was a bad influence, but Syed would never lie to me like that. He would never betray his family. He would never betray God.

When I was walking home from school yesterday I saw Syed saying goodbye to Connor just outside our house. He was laughing, and I felt a pang in my chest. He never laughed like that around me any more.

Connor was red in the face. It clashed horribly with his whitish-blond hair, and I allowed myself a smirk, even though it was really no consolation. He pulled away from Syed, and Syed grabbed his wrist and yanked him back. I could almost hear them, Connor made an irritated little grunt – but he didn't look too upset. Syed grinned cheekily up at him. I was all set to march right up to them and force them apart.

But then Syed wrapped his arms around Connor's neck and raised his head. His head tilted to one side as his face neared his friend's. Just his friend. Just his best friend. Then Connor turned and carried on walking down the street, and Syed waved to him.

As if nothing had happened. It was only when he managed to drag his eyes away from Connor that he saw me staring at him, my heart pounding and my blood like ice in my veins. He didn't say anything to me. He just gave me a small, sheepish smile and made his way up the garden path and opened the front door, leaving me alone in the street. It couldn't have been what I thought it was. If it had, wouldn't Syed have tried to explain? To beg me for forgiveness? I was sixteen. I was the oldest and cleverest of all my friends. But it must have been my imagination. After all, Syed would never do that to me. My brother, the same boy who had played dolls with me and pretended to be my date at every dance, would never do such a dirty, hurtful thing. In a few years, he would marry the woman Mum and Dad picked out for him and they would have children and be happy. And I'd be happy, too.

The following morning, Syed asked me quietly not to tell Mum and Dad.

I told him I didn't know what he was talking about.

Grandad By Alex Harker

I'm his recent past.
Kept behind one of his locked doors,
He doesn't remember me anymore
For now I'm just a stranger
A new face, a new voice.

How can you tell a person
Who doesn't recognise you,
That you love him and always will?

He always treated me well,
Looked after me when I was down
Accepted our family, as his own.
Now he doesn't even recognise me.
I never want to end like that.
I never want to grow old,
I don't want to forget my loved ones
And lose my soul.

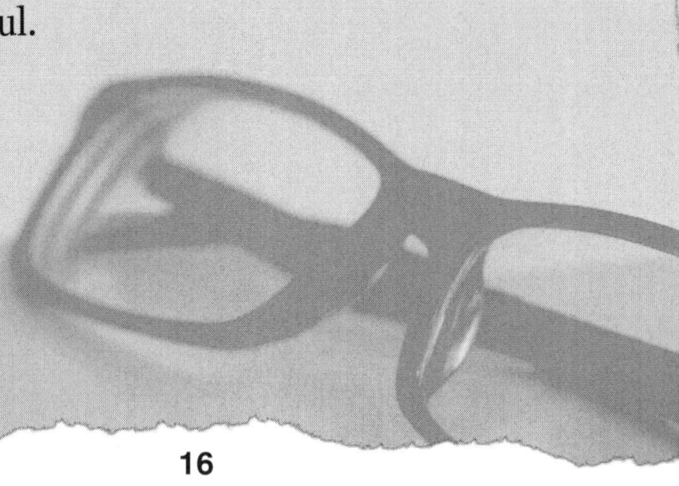

EVELYN AND THE BISCUIT TIN

By Robyn Ollett

This room is not too nice.
The walls are a horrid salmon pink.
I need some Garibaldi's
And some time to think.

Remember that flick with Barbara
The one who always sobs;
I'd be far more composed than that.
I'm only upset by Hobnobs.

I wish something would happen soon,
Now let's move on to the shortbread,
I'm sure I'd be the last one alive
Just me and The Living Dead.

Forever, I'd sit, smelling like biscuits
And not of rancid rotten flesh and skin.
The infected Walking Dead that groan,
Stuck on earth like you in your tin.

Sorry dear, if I'm boring you.
Have a chocolate digestive sweetie,
Just wait 'till you're dunked and drowned,
And I'll sit here with my sweet tea.

Crumbs! I'm not saying I'm immortal!
Or that I'm skilled in the deadly arts,
But nothing would care to chew me up
In The Land of the Dead, un-beating hearts.

I wish you would eat your party ring.
Are you just going to stare at it forever?
I've got a theory that your brain is mush.
Dead Silence. You think you're so clever.

Now I do not want to raise my voice.
You insist on making my stomach sour!
'They're coming to get you,' is what he said,
And we'll all perish within the hour.

REMEMBER THY YOUTH

by JohnPaul Melling

I look around. A beautiful field
Peace and serenity. The whispering rape
Laughs absent-mindedly at the oncoming cars.

Return home now my dearest boy
My father's whispering call
Your mind runs free and sows the soul
Unto each God's heavenly plants.

You climb the wall and hum with the bees
Lay yourself down and drift off to sleep
Dream of the rabbits, pheasants and sheep
Laying beside you, alone in the crop.

Smell that sweet hay, the luscious tree blossom
Takes you back to the days of your youth
With mud on your knee, an apple in hand
The sun shining down as you open your eyes.

I look around. A beautiful field
Peace and serenity. The whispering rape
I lift up my thumb at the oncoming cars.

This Can't Last (But I Wish It Could)

By Anna Twizell

Strumming away around the flames,
With the beauty that time seems to stop,
You bow your head and close your eyes,
The cold wind's breeze nips my skin,
This can't last but I wish it could.

When I'm with you I feel no blame,
Relaxation – my pulse just drops,
I smell burning, see fireflies,
The heat is scaring away our sin,
This can't last but I wish it could.

I'll Stand By You

My prophecy has been foreseen
I am the protection you never see,
I'm the guardian angel on your back
Always ready to protect and attack.
I'll keep you safe from the darkness
To keep you truly clueless,
To hide you from the anarchy behind
I'm sorry for keeping you so blind.

I'm your protection that never slacks,
My strength and potential never seem to lack.
For I will always be there on your back,
Protecting you from any attack
I promise you I'll always be here
Protecting you forever, my dear.
Whenever you're in need
I'll always be there,
To hide you under my wing of eternal care.

You are my only one
For whom I care,
I promise you
I'll always be there.
No matter how,
No matter where
I'll always be there.

However, love has got to be set free,
So take my hand and follow me.
I'll show you the word,
I'll open your eyes
So you can see the whole world lies.

I'll hide you from criticism,
They'll never understand
People like you and me
Are banned from this land.
So forever here I'll be stood,
With an outstretched hand,
Waiting forever on the border between lands.

By Alex Harker

DAUNTLESS DAVE RULEZ!!

DAUNTLESS DAVE AND THE DEVILISHLY DAZZLING DUDE WHO DOOMS DASTARDLY DUDES

Back in 2007, a lumber factory in New Jersey USA caught fire. Luckily, I was working there at the time so I got to experience the first epic thing that's ever happened in my craptacular life. A sinister being of ultimate bastardness wanted to burn down the lumber factory, whilst slaughtering all us innocent workers in the process. He basically launched an assault using his fire powers to burn us all down. I won't lie to you. I was shitting myself, don't judge me! Anybody in the presence of The Dark Lord of Flame was in instant danger!

But then, a mighty looking silhouette showed up in front of all us thousands that were trapped in the burning lumber factory. It walked forward to reveal the incredibly heroic (and handsome) figure of a man, and what a man. Tall yet muscular, and sporting what any self respecting internationally famous super hero would wear, spandex, coloured with the heroic mix of red and gold. Anyway, once we saw the legendary hero, Ultra Dude, we had a glimpse of hope.

Ultra Dude evacuated everybody with his psychic powers, except me, I was immune for reasons to be revealed later, anyway, the two super power humans clashed. After epically colliding in a manner which was epically epic, both super heroes were pushed back a few feet due to the force of the impact. There was an intense stare down between the two, one a warrior of justice, the other a bringer of death and darkness. I heard they used to be the closest most inseparable friends, who did everything together, I mean EVERYTHING, things that I cannot mention in case a child decides to read this. So they used to be the ultimate super hero lovers, as happy as can be. Until The Dark Lord of Flame accidentally massacred Ultra Dude's family using his fire powers of doom. Ultra Dude has sworn his revenge since.

I stood in awe as they stared each other down, ready to start their battle of destiny. Ultra Dude fired a laser beam out of his nipple and killed the flame guy instantly. It was awesome! His nipple was like," pew pew," and Dark Lord of Flame was like, "UWARGH!" and stuff. So after all that, I remembered that I was suffocating because of the smoke and stuff so I passed out.

Then I woke up with the world's sexiest hero standing in front of me. I was strapped to a chair in what appeared to be Ultra Dude's ultra secret ultra awesome ultra mega super fantastic ultra rare secret base of awesomeness. For some reason it kinda turned me on. He started glaring at me with his furious eyes of glory, which have the power to make anybody that look into them spurt out the truth so I screamed, "I AM VERY TURNED ON RIGHT NOW! YOU ARE MY IDOL! I WANT TO BE YOUR SLAVE!!!!!!"

And that's how I became the sidekick of Ultra Dude.

By Sam Johnson !!

The Man in Red

Have you ever wondered about the man in red?
The one who sneaks when you're tucked in bed.
The one with a beard so white.
His stomach packed into his suit so tight.
Where does he come from? You may wonder.
It's somewhere from below.... Way down under.
Where the demons hiss and the lava burns.
A shadowy figure appears and turns.
The prince of darkness himself, the one they call Satan.
Every Christmas squeezed into a suit that's straightened.
With boots as black as night,
And a beaming smile so bright.
All the reindeers lined up in a row,
Running though boiling lava to freezing snow.
Yes, the one you all love so well,
Saint Nick, Santa Claus bids the underworld farewell.
To deliver joy to children of all,
Every Tom, Peter and Paul.
All except the son of one,
Who perished on the cross... and is long gone.
Christmas was once his, I hear,
Rejoicing his name year after year.
Satan grew jealous of the saviour's love.
So he disguised himself from the world above,
Changing his name to suit the situation.
Now he takes off into the skies, flying from nation to nation,
Ridding the celebration of the Son of God,
Under the name Santa. What a deceiving sod!

By James Phoenix

THE BEAUTY OF THE HUMAN RACE

I had a friend called Mickey
Such a nice guy,
Ask him anything and he'd never tell a lie.
That's until you asked about his parents,
He'd go really shy.

He'd turn on heel and run back home
And cry in his room all alone,
Until his mum and dad got back
And threatened to give him a smack.
He never got in their way,
Always doing what they say.

He didn't know you could live any other way.
Thought everyone had to live like this
Afraid to leave his room for even an innocent piss,
Cos he'd had to walk past the front room
Where his mother always sat.
He'd have to hold it in, and wait 'till she was busy
And scamper past like an unwanted rat.

Food was out of the question for Mickey
He'd only get the scraps
Barely enough to live on
And not enough to fight back
For he was on the edge of death
Always fearing the threat of a whack.

The belt still made him shiver
Marks on his back were very plain
Showing his hideous pain
But he realised the worst was still to come,
He hadn't felt his dad's cane.

He needed a way to escape
To simply get away,
He knew he somehow would
But he'd have to wait another day.

His dad had friends over this time
And he had to stay in his room,
He was promised some food later
Probably some leftover slime.

They both showed no mercy
To their own flesh and blood.
If anyone ever asked what happened
They'd always say "he fell in the mud",
It was always clumsy Mickey.

One day on the way back from school
He saw a father and son;
They were playing on the field
Just generally having fun.
Sudden realisation came to Mickey
He realised all this bad must be undone.

Mickey ran home,
And burst through the door.
Went straight to the kitchen
And straight to the drawer.
He opened it up and pulled out a knife,
He ran to the living room
Brandishing his weapon.

This angered his dad
It made him real mad,
He desperately ran and hid
But soon was found.
He was just an innocent kid!

His dad wouldn't stop
The belt hitting down
Right on his crown.
His body thudded
Straight to the ground,

But this didn't stop him
His dad fought on,
Mickey screaming in pain,
And with nothing to gain,
He fought his dad
And let out all his hatred.

"Go fuck yourself!"
His dad still swung,
Bursting out laughing.
In came his mum,
She joined the fight
But not for the boy,
She got out a new little toy.
His dad's old cane,
Mickey winced in pain.

His body lay on the floor,
Lifeless next to the door.
The police were called
But no body was found,
It was buried 6 feet under ground.

By Alex Harker

THROUGH GLOVES

BY ROBYN OLLETT

I could only feel you a little bit.
I could hear your muffled scream.
I could hear a muted choke.
I could see your face screw up.
I could see your eyes close tight.
I could smell salt.
I could taste hate.
But I could only feel you a little bit.

I couldn't feel anything anymore.
I couldn't hear a pulse.
I couldn't see any movement.
I couldn't feel breathing.
I couldn't see red.
I couldn't smell the warmth.
I couldn't hear any cries.
So, I couldn't feel anything anymore.

The Brown, Leather Bracelet

Blood looks worse in the snow.

Drip… **Drip**… **Drip**… Why did he pick me?

Ten years ago. School. We ran together. Ran from the name calling. It was always worse for him. He cried and I comforted. So many times…

Five years ago. College. He didn't speak to me. I was lucky; my looks took me far. His didn't. Secret Santa. No one wanted him, but I got him. I made him a bracelet out of brown leather. He put it straight on.

Three years ago. University. I didn't know where he went. Nights out, essays, lectures, reading; I did not have time for him and I forgot him.

Today. Winter. Christmas Day and I went for my annual walk in the snow. To help me relax. I passed one man. He stared at me. A drop of pity fell from my mind as I walked by him. I did not remember him at first. I turned round and saw him staring at me. He is homeless now. He said the snow is cold. "Obviously", I thought. He wished me a Merry Christmas and stabbed me with the hand wearing the bracelet that I had made him five years ago.

Blood looks worse in the snow.

By Helen Daly

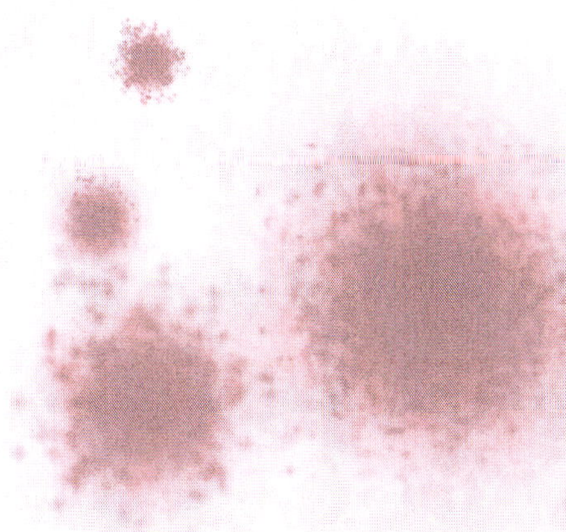

It's almost midnight. My shift was over more than an hour ago, but what do I have to get home to? A mouldy flat, a cuppa soup while huddled under the duvet. Central heating went tits up months ago, and there's no way I'm going to hire someone who can barely speak English to fix it. That's all there is to London nowadays. If it isn't an obnoxious twenty-something-year-old who wouldn't know a hard day's work if it bit him on his Calvin Klein-clad arse lumping himself into the back seat, it's an 'economical migrant', or a naive tourist who announces the name of an authentic-sounding pub with a self-satisfied smile, as if they too are a part of the daily stream of middle-class citizens, and somehow belong in a crumbling dive, eating pathetic mash made from half-fat milk and powder with sausages the Saturday staff had picked up that morning from Tesco.

I decide to do one last round before packing in for the night. It's never too hard to find someone in need of a lift. The old ale houses close up at eleven and the fruits of their labours can often be found staggering aimlessly, jeering and vomiting and pissing on the poor homeless sod who's trying to sell them a Big Issue.

I park in my usual spot. It's ten minutes, longer than usual, until someone hauls the back door open and bundles a half-conscious young man inside before letting rip some unintelligible slur and slamming the door shut again. I adjust my mirror and observe the man sprawled out on the torn, stinking seats. On a good day, he might look respectable: short, sensibly-cut brown hair and the slightest trace of a beard. Right now he doesn't look fit to lick the poor homeless sod's turd-soaked shoes.

"Where to, mate?" I ask.

He groans and wriggles onto his front so that his face is squashed against the seats. I start the engine and pull away from the curb. He's not bad looking, I decide. It'd be difficult to top last night's, a tall, brown-breasted blonde with legs up to here. A little thrill jolts through me as I recall her long neck and how her glossy pink lips had quivered just so.

The people I pick up, they're all the same really. Pretentious twats who're too absorbed in their own cushy little lives to focus on anything but. I know what they see when they look at me: a sad, fat old man, pushing fifty and with nothing to show for it except the stains on his shirt and the calluses on his hands. What do they know? I'm more than that. I'm cleverer than that. Cleverer than them.

Behind me, the man has somehow managed to heave himself into a sitting position, forehead pressed against the window and thudding along with every bump in the road. His eyes are bulging and fixed straight ahead. It won't surprise me if he's high on pot or crack or some other not-quite-legal substance.

"Rough night?" I say.

The man gurgles and through my mirror I see his head tip back, exposing his throat. It's surprisingly pale and slender. He keeps swallowing, probably forcing down a mouthful of puke, and his Adam's apple dips every time. Small jolts of electricity run through my body.

My hands grow clammy in anticipation and stick to the wheel as I turn into a quiet street. Beads of sweat glisten on my forehead under the flicker of the dim street-lamps that line the pavement. I pull up. The handbrake grinds horribly. That couldn't be good for the brakes; I make a mental note to inform Steve over a pint later.

I shift in my seat, straining my neck to look at the man behind me. He barely even blinks. Not that they ever do. I'm not a person to them. I'm a machine, an invisible ghost of a presence who only exists while they're in my car, and then only to take them to where they want to be. They get out; I disappear.

I unstrap my seat belt. The man's eyes flicker towards me; I can tell he's coming to.

"What's your name?" I ask.

"Jason," he replies. His voice is hazy. Distant. Trusting.

I take the wire out of my pocket.

By Amy Holmes

OBSESSIONS

By Steph Mitchell

It started out so small, I do confess,
all I wanted to do was to get inside that pretty little dress.
I worked so very hard, every night and every day,
It's those painful memories that I just wish would go away.
The horrible ordeals I put myself through,
I do regret.
Unfortunately I will have to live with it.
Never to forget.
I know now that there are no reasons to cry,
nor to shout.
I guess my secret isn't so "deep and dark"
and is finally coming out.
It's not so well hidden: every regret.
Part of my life I could live without.

Duchess

There she is again. Wonder if she'll notice me this time, if she can pull her attention from that fancy man she's clinging onto. There they go, waltzing into another fine jewellery store, her fingers becoming encrusted in even more sparkling diamonds… blue like my heart. I can't buy you riches of gold or gems, fine silks or sprawling mansions. But tell me, does he give you what you need? Not want, but need? Does he shower you in everlasting affection? Does he hold you so close to him that your hearts become one? I would. You could be my everything and I could be yours. So I'll keep on waiting, my lady, and hope that our two worlds unite. Until then I'll be there to clean away your sorrows, to tidy away your fears and doubts, as your loyal, loyal servant, my lady.

By James Phoenix

SUMMER RAIN

Two roses sway, their soft petals meet
Warm rain caresses, a light soothing heat
Summer rain ends now, autumn is nigh
A break for the winter, in the snow we must die
So parting for now but soon we will greet.

The harsh winter fades, He now sees the sky
"Just wait 'till the snow melts", he tries not to cry
But will he see his rose pure red?
Their time apart was like being dead
Thinking of her now, time starts to fly.

The snow is now gone, spring then brings life
Looking around I see we flora are rife
Push out from the ground, Dear. I've missed you so much
But three shoots lay earthbound and I cannot touch
The foxglove then says, "Will you please be my wife?"

Three flowers sway, he begs her again
He's down on his knees, he feels like he's slain
She looks back at him, his petals have withered
Picks up her bags and gets onto the train
He's left on the platform in that cold summer rain.

By JohnPaul Melling

Ignorance

By Alex Harker

Finally open your eyes,
You can't see the real world,
Through all those lies,
Let me free your soul.

They say ignorance is bliss,
Hiding yourself deep in that mist.
Staying in that spot forever,
Replaying that first kiss.

AMATERASU

I am the rising sun, the crescent moon,
The reflecting light off a distant ocean,
Flowers bow as I make my way across the land,
Each stride giving birth to new life, new souls, new colours.
The land once vibrant and beautiful, the crimson roses and warming greens,
Has been soiled by evil; creatures of the night now walking the land of the holy.
The majestic trees that once stood, each branch an age old, each with a story to tell,
Now stand darkened, a shadow of their former selves,
No life, no soul, no colour.
The world wasn't always this way,
The golden land of Nippon was once a masterpiece of transcendent glory,
Children playing in the lustrous gleaming fields of pink and indigo,
Waterfalls drifting gracefully into pools of wondrous, shining aqua.
All was peaceful. But then he arrived.

Orochi. The eight-headed dragon of the underworld awoke,
And the beauty of the world was shrouded in darkness,
With each roar the colour drained from the land,
The people grew sad and prayed to the heavens for a saviour.
I answered that call.
As I shake my snow-white fur, the ground ignites in a warming glow,
Leaving behind the seeds of life, restoring grace to the dead floors of Nippon,
I howl at the newborn moon and listen carefully,
The trees of old are gaining back their ancient marvel,
But my work here is far from over.
I must prepare for battle, as this world's protector and restorer,
To repel evil and bestow the beauty that was robbed from the world,
So away I pounce, flowers spout from my gentle paws,
Rushing through fields of jewels, mountains of ice cold blue,
Ready to face the evil over the next fading horizon.

By James Phoenix

I Doubt In Thee Lord

The Angels cry and weep
Heart heavy in defeat.
They fight to keep heaven pure
But who really does possess the cure,
For the perfect human,
The perfect being?

If God is so perfect
Yet created us all,
How did he allow us to fall?
Since he created this world
And all it possesses,
He has made all the bad,
All the evil, all the sin.
Why didn't he just start again,
And throw the rubbish in the bin?

He made the "perfect world"
To watch and observe,
What purpose is this meant to serve?
Are we supposed to live these lives?
To simply be judged by a being higher than ours,
For him to pick out all our flaws,

What gives him the right to hold onto such power?
We know nothing about this man
Yet we trust him so much,
He just seems to have us all within his clutch.
The people of this world
Are shifting on the learning curve.
People are gaining they're own thoughts,
Seeing the world in their own eyes.

Who's to say God and Buddha are wrong?
Going to school singing those same Christian songs,
Why should we be forced into something,
In which we don't believe?
If God wanted free will,
Surely this is not his way.
Just take the pill, my son,
Everything will be okay.

By Alex Harker

DAUNTLESS DAVE is AWESOME!!!

A few days after the last chapter, which was actually quite crappy to be completely honest, I began my awesome sidekick training of justice and stuff. First step of training was by far the most vital step of any hero. The super suit! Ultra Dude heroically logged in on his awesome eBay account and found a hip and funky costume, a red morph suit with the initials "DD" written in pink inside a black love heart. It was glorious. Found at a very reasonable price as well, the world is a better place with eBay. Arrived within two working days and it came in good condition.

Second step of sidekick training was ass kicking, Ultra Dude has the power to unlock the powers of people and stuff so he put his index finger into my ear and then I guess I got super powers. I CAN F_CKING FLY! I HAVE SUPER HUMAN F_CKING STRENGTH! I CAN TURN INTO A LEAF. I CAN USE MY BRAIN TO MOVE STUFF! I AM F_CKING AWESOME!!!! I got used to these powers by beating up a bunch of old dudes. This was fun. My training was nearly complete!

I thought perhaps the love of my life, Ultra Dude, would take me seriously and maybe make out with me and stuff. He called me in to his lair of ultra awesomeness for my last step of training.

"Are you ready to do the final task in becoming worthy of becoming my sidekick?"

"YES! I WILL ALWAYS BE READY TO DO ANYTHING FOR YOU ULTRA DUDE, MY LOVE! YOU STILL TURN ME ON AND I HAVE SEXUAL DREAMS ABOUT YOU EVERY NIGHT!"

"I hate my eyes of truth sometimes, anyway, your task is to stop this kid from falling to his death" He pulled out some kid from out of what seemed like nowhere then threw him out the window, which meant a 300ft drop. "Well, err, you gonna go get him?"

"Oh Right! Yeah." I flew out the window to go get him but he landed and died. Bummer.

"Good job! You pass! That kid was evil and smelt like vinegar! You are now my sidekick!"

Yaaaaaaaaaaaaay!!!!

Now that my training was finally over, I was ready to fight crime and stuff, I had become super sidekick extraordinaire. I became Dauntless Dave!™ Ultra Dude took me on our first crime fighting adventure. A mysterious villian has been seen harassing children. We arrived, only to be greeted by the most terrifying being in the entire universe...

By Sam Johnson

FAIRY TALE ELECTION

Once upon a time, in a magical far away land,
There were three greedy men, with the country at hand,
Thursday 6th May, the general election arrived,
Nick, David and Gordon, were taking it in their stride.
The primary colours blazed; yellow, blue and red,
The fuss people made, you'd think someone was dead.
Nick was clad in yellow, with his sword down by his side,
David held up a blue shield, to protect his manly pride,
Gordon took to hiding, he quivered in his red boots,
He was too afraid to face these nasty sorts of brutes.
Was it going to be a majority? Or maybe even a hung?
For the type of business, Nick and David were too young.
All three of the men wanted to win, so they could take control,
Each thought they could to a better job, even if it
meant sacrificing a soul,
The townsfolk were in suspense, every creature had to vote,
Giants, elves, fairies went to polling stations, to
keep the land afloat.
The army called the Tories thought that their
victory would prevail,
They knew if they could have full charge that they
would never fail,
The reds were lacking drastically, they know they'd
lost their chance,
So Gordon took a backseat, to let the blues advance.
David had the evil Queen's word, meaning victory he
could pursue,
Tuesday 11th of May, he turned the far away land blue.

BY ANNA TWIZELL

THE CAT IN THE NIGHT-TIME

By JohnPaul Melling

BANG…arch your back
Show no fear, dear little one
It's but only our door
Conquer the enemy, my nocturnal beauty

Black cat howls
The whisper of evil
Eyes that pierce
The deepest part of the soul

Delicate hunter
Out in the streets
Cry as you gaze up
At the glistening moon

Scratch, bite and pounce
My beautiful lioness
Show them your power
As you stalk the streets this night
Rest not till you reach the gate to our door

Now let there be light
The heavens aglow
The sun rises up, dispel the fear
Darkness is gone but so is she
She knows it is over, at least for the night
She's gone in a howl of the wind

Back home now my mysterious cat
Open the door; come into the warmth
Sleep now, warm in your bed
Sleep until later when the moon is full
We'll see each other soon…real soon

Folk Song in Prose

Today is summer solstice and I am in a fairy circle; a ring of toadstools big and small, sprouting up between the daisies and poppies. All weeds and fungus but in the hazy light, scattered with floating pollen boats, the mind plays tricks so all are pearls and jewels. If I were born from the mud, like you fine folk, I would be a ruby; so small I'd be mistaken for a pomegranate seed and be carried off by a hungry blackbird. The view from her skyward stealing would be splendid, but for now I'm quite happy to look at beautiful things from the ground for I'm a simple pebble with no glistening petals.

By Robyn Ollett

To live...

I'm walking.
Not sure where; I'll know when I arrive.
I'm smelling.
The fresh scent of grass, the flowers, the air.
I'm seeing.
The patterns of pinks, greens and blue. All moulding into one. Together.
I'm breathing.
The cool, calming air. Reassuring. Soothing
I'm thinking.
About yesterday, about the long path ahead.
I'm touching.
The soft petals, glistening with mildew; yet they are not cold, no, so warm.
I'm listening.
To the melody of this path I walk. Silence.
I'm living.

By Helen Daly

Dear Diary
By Steph Mitchell

Dear diary, I know it's been a long time now
but Ana's back and stronger, I just don't know how
I thought I could fight her off, I thought I'd be safe
but all that Ana makes me want is a Tiny Waist

Dear diary, Ana has done all she can
but all she managed was to lose 8 pounds
I'm really worried now Mia is comin' back
every time I eat Mia is prepared to attack

Dear diary, Mia is vicious again
I can't even sit and eat lunch with my friends
her acid tongue and high demand are just too much to take
I'm becoming another Media Whore, or maybe just a Fake

Dear diary, Mia brought me down to
my ideal weight today
but now I can't stop
much to my friend's dismay
Shrinking and shrinking
hiding what I'm becoming
hiding myself away.

The Future's What's Important!

Everyone wants to be remembered for what they've done,
But what have I left behind for people to remember me by?
A bunch of mistakes, this is my time to go, to run.
I am just a boy, seeing the world through my eyes,
Watching and waiting, seeing my end come to on nigh.
This is my way of screaming for help, to be remembered
For who I am, not for what I did.

When my true meaning arrives
Don't try to judge me on my past,
Judge me on what I'm doing now.
This shall be my main objective and my last.
Remember the good, not the bad.
Meanings must be complete, but at what cost?
If I am to go in order to save others,
I would give my life for all my sisters and brothers.

By Alex Harker

A Sea Dog's Christmas

Y'argh. Ye don't what know it be like, livin' the life of a pirate! Thar be the sweet things, like drinkin', stealin', pillagin', burnin', rapin', murderin', rapin', an' sewin'. But thar be one time of Yar that really yanks me beard. It be that Christmas time of Yar. Everyone be singin' and sharin' merriment. Where I can't do a blasted thing about it! Because me useless bastard ship be getting trapped in all the ice! Me 'n' me crew be stuck rapin' and burnin' each other on the ship because thar be no village in sight. It sickens me old black heart. Thar be men, women and children all giddy with thar families and here I be, wimme crew, livin' on frozen fish guts 'n' our own piss. Me belly be achin' for the blood 'n' rum of them spoilt landlubbers. Thar'll be sorry, once this accursed ship gets movin' again, me 'n' me crew'll rape up a storm!

By Sam Johnson

The Hectic Caterer

Why hello you,
Just come on through,
Remove your shoe,
I'm making stew,
Should it be blue?
Oh what to do!
D'you think they'll sue?
Then just on cue,
I thought 'oh geeez!',
Forgot the peas,
And the goat's cheese,
They'll surely tease,
About my pleas,
I'm on my knees,
With such a wheeze,
I'm going to sneeze!
I need my bed,
I've always said,
Men must be fed,
But all this dread,
My fingers are red,
From kneading the bread,
I'm losing my head!
Lock me in the shed.
Oh God oh why,
Although I try,
I've burnt the pie!
And scalded my thigh,
I'm feeling high,
Just like a fly,
Up in the sky.
I need to buy,
A spicy dip,
I'm gonna flip,
Must get a grip!
I need a kip,
Or maybe a trip,
Possibly a sneaky sip,
A morphine drip?
Ouch! I've bit my lip.

By Anna Twizell

Red, Red Wine

You tease my lips with such great taste
And rush into my blood with such fast haste.
You cheer me up like a kiss from above
And fill my heart so full of love.

You give me a different view to life
Although a little dizzy and bizarre,
You make even the ugliest,
Look like a star.

You give me confidence
And broaden my smile.
You hide all my feelings
And make it worthwhile.

Your crimson mystery goes down a treat,
Makes me dizzy and light on my feet.
Whilst I pretend to be discrete
But your happiness is hard to hide.
It burns to escape from the inside,
It erupts in a slur or collapses to the floor.
By morning time you bring me pain
Any noise makes my head sore.
All my muscles ache again and again.

All morning with my head in the sink
I knew I shouldn't have had that drink.
By evening I'll be fine
Ready to start once again on the wine.

By Alex Harker

SUNNY DAY

By Sam Johnson

It was a typical day on the famous street. Children were playing, cute furry monsters sang and a giant yellow bird was having a great time on his roller blades, as birds do. The cute little red monster followed the street's weekly thingy of teaching little kiddies stuff about life. Today they did colours, which the happy little monsters loved so much because they are all ever so colourful and pretty so they wished to present their magnificent blues, oranges, yellows and reds. It all started out well.

"Me blue!" the greedy blue monster said, "That same color as sky! But not same as COOKIES!" He then started eating a bunch of yummy cookies.

The smallest cute silly little red monster stood up to the centre of their little color game.

"I'm red! That same color as...umm..." The little red monster walked around to help him think about what was red, but had a nasty tumble. Strange red water started spilling from the little red monster's knee.

"Oh what's this? This is red!" said the little red monster with excitement.

"Ooooh! Let me see!" said the little purple man with pointy teeth. He got a small drop of this strange new water and gave it a taste. "It is delicious! MWAH HAH HAH!" He bit a bigger hole into the little red monster's throat and drank more.

"Let me try some too!"

"Leave some for me!"

Soon enough, the little red monster was eaten all up. He had an annoying voice anyway, and besides, everyone was full and happy, except for the little purple man with sharp teeth. He looked different.

"MORE!" he shouted. He leaped on a nearby girl who joined in on their fun little color game and bit her cute face off and enjoyed another yummy snack, and another and another.

Soon enough there were no more kids and no more grownups. The little purple man with the sharp teeth was very fond of these people and he felt very, very bad. So the sad purple man locked himself away for the rest of his days.

The crazy old blue monster was very sad about this, so he went to the one thing that kept him happy. He ate cookies, tons and tons of cookies, day by day, year by year, the monster aged and got fatter and fatter until his frail old body could take no more. There were no people left alive by then, just a few silly little monsters and a giant featherless bird hanging from his neck off a clothes line. He got very, very sad because a friend went to sleep forever and so he plucked out all his feathers and tied a string around his neck and tried to fly, silly bird.

The street became a nice business place for some bad people. They sold sugar and pretty little mushrooms and those pointy things the doctors put in us before letting us have a lollipop.

They used their bad toys that go bang on some of the sad little monsters as they fed off whatever animal they could find. Sometimes the bad men would make their toys go bang on each other. There was a lot of that red water which the silly little monsters loved ever so much. The nice policemen came along one day and used their toys that go bang until all the bad men dropped down in their own red water.

There was nothing on this lovely street anymore, except in a certain trashcan. There was a grouchy green monster in it; he sat in his nice little home alone, smiling, which was weird because he was always grouchy when the other funny little monsters were around. All that could be heard in the street was the faintest echo of laughter and a distorted little tune with some singing; you just could make out how the song went:

"Sunny Day, sweepin' the clouds away. On my way to where the air is sweet..."

DAUNTLESS DAVE VS A DASTARDLY DEVIANT

The one villain in the entire universe who could stand up to Ultra Dude stood before us. It was an elderly woman, in a green floral dress with a bosom covered in titanium, sporting green tinted shades and grey hair, spiked up at least 4ft high. She was wielding two walking sticks, both glowing red. She was THE WRINKLED MENACE accompanied by her haunted floating nighty sidekick, THE MIGHTY NIGHTY! Ultra Dude, having a secret phobia of the elderly, curled up into a ball and started crying and wetting himself, so it was up to me to stop this Wrinkled Menace. She slammed her titanium bosoms into Ultra Dude and sent him flying because she's a bitch like that. I wet myself. But I had to help protect the children that she was calling names and throwing paper cups of doom at. She hit me in the face with one of her sticks and I was out.

When I (awesomely) woke up, I was chained up to a wall in this little pink room, which smelt of cat pee. Tthere was some ugly kid chained up next to me. The Wrinkled Menace stood there smiling at me.

"Now that I have captured you, Dumb-ass Dave, Ultra Dude is defenseless against my wrath. He has only been able to defeat me because he's always had a sidekick, and you're crap, so I win. LOL. Now before I end you with my glorious breasts, I will insult this child!"

It was unbearable; she was using the most offensive insults she could come up with.

"I had sexual relations with your mother! Your mother moans like a bitch! You're ugly and smell of cotton!" She then threw a paper cup at him.

THAT CROSSED THE LINE!

I started pulsing with energy, my nipples went hard as bullets and I felt powerful. The chains broke away and I then commenced with the ass kicking. I immediately kicked her in the balls. But it wasn't very effective! It was like she didn't have balls or something! She must be an alien! :O She performed a counter attack with her breasts shouting:

"FEEL THE WRATH OF MY CHESTICLES!"

I did an awesome duck and did a Shoryuken like Ryu from Street Fighter but punched her boob and hurt my hand, I might have cried a bit but I'm super manly so I only cried for about 6 seconds. She went to do a swipe at me with one of her glowy stick things, but put her back out and couldn't move. We were truly evenly matched. I had found my arch nemesis. I took advantage of the situation and pushed her over and I was victorious! I freed the ugly kid and turned him loose to make his own way out; he was freaking me out a bit because he was so ugly.

As I went to make my exit, The Mighty Nighty appeared from out of the shadows, but caught fire on a candle and sort of just burnt away so that wasn't really much of a problem. I flew away victorious and met with Ultra Dude about my awesome victory.

"Good job, Dauntless Dave! It's good to hear The Wrinkled Menace is behind bars!"

....I sort of forgot about that part...

FFFFFFFFFFFFFUUUUUUUUUUUUUUUUUUUUUUUUUUUUUU-

<<A message from the Wrinkled Menace>>

DAVE! YOU STUPID LITTLE BOY! LETTING ME AND MY MENACING INSULTS AND PAPER CUPS WALK FREE! NEXT TIME WE MEET I WILL HAVE MY REVENGE! MWAAAHAHAHAHAHAHAHAHAHAHAAAAAA!!! (I wrote down how I laugh so you get the idea of how amused I am.)

That's the beginning of my sexy story! Will I find my love with Ultra Dude? Will I defeat more deadly villains? And how many more boob-related things will happen?

FIND OUT IN THE NEXT EXCITING-ISH CHAPTER OF DAUNTLESS DAVE! OUT WHEN THE INCREDIBLY HANDSOME WRITER FEELS LIKE IT.

By Sam Johnson

THE RE-GENESIS OF EVE

She walks to the field, the blossoming tree
bearing the fruit that called to her soul
delicious temptation, red as the rose
small, ripe and delicate, savour the touch

Sensuous beauty, fruit of the divine
fall of the feminine, birth of holy wrath
whisper to me, call my desire
reach out!
touch that one forbidden love

Draw me towards the luscious sweet fruit
penetrate, the honey-sweet juice
but wait…what do I feel?
sweetness to sour, a bitter sting in my mouth

My breath becomes still
my pulse becomes weak
venomous liquids burn and weep in my veins

She falls down to hell, the apple in hand
time has not forgotten the temptation of sin
He looks down and cries,
an oncoming rain.

By JohnPaul Melling